PACIFIC COAST

A Panoramic Postcard Book

by Thea Schrack

D0885210

CHRONICLE BOOKS

Mendocino Coast, California

1st class
POSTAGE

COPYRIGHT © 1999 THEA SCHRACK/FROM *PACIFIC COAST: A PANORAMIC POSTCARD BOOK*, PUBLISHED BY CHRONICLE BOOKS.

Ruby Beach, Washington

1st class
POSTAGE

COPYRIGHT © 1999 THEA SCHRACK/FROM *PACIFIC COAST: A PANORAMIC POSTCARD BOOK*, PUBLISHED BY CHRONICLE BOOKS.

Mission Beach, San Diego, California

1st class
POSTAGE

COPYRIGHT © 1999 THEA SCHRACK/FROM *PACIFIC COAST: A PANORAMIC POSTCARD BOOK,* PUBLISHED BY CHRONICLE BOOKS.

Central Oregon Coast

1st class
POSTAGE

COPYRIGHT © 1999 THEA SCHRACK/FROM *PACIFIC COAST: A PANORAMIC POSTCARD BOOK*, PUBLISHED BY CHRONICLE BOOKS.

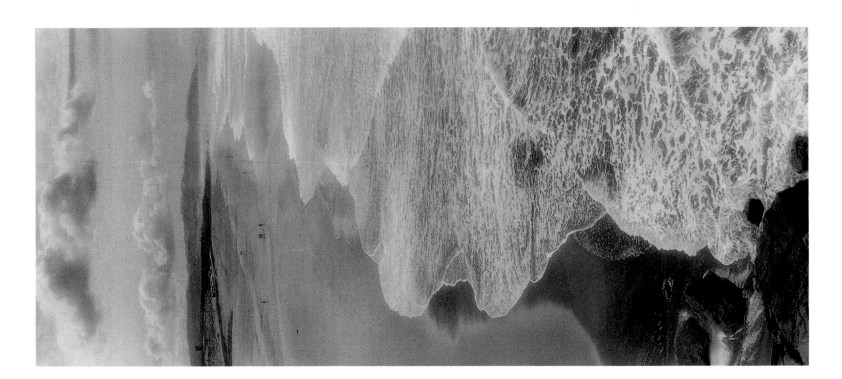

Ocean Beach, San Francisco, California

1st class
POSTAGE

COPYRIGHT © 1999 THEA SCHRACK/FROM *PACIFIC COAST: A PANORAMIC POSTCARD BOOK*, PUBLISHED BY CHRONICLE BOOKS.

Doe Bay, Orcas Island, San Juan Islands, Washington

1st class
POSTAGE

COPYRIGHT © 1999 THEA SCHRACK/FROM *PACIFIC COAST: A PANORAMIC POSTCARD BOOK*, PUBLISHED BY CHRONICLE BOOKS.

Julia Pfeiffer Burns State Park, Big Sur, California

1st class
POSTAGE

COPYRIGHT © 1999 THEA SCHRACK/FROM *PACIFIC COAST: A PANORAMIC POSTCARD BOOK,* PUBLISHED BY CHRONICLE BOOKS.

Santa Monica, California

1st class
POSTAGE

COPYRIGHT © 1999 THEA SCHRACK/FROM *PACIFIC COAST: A PANORAMIC POSTCARD BOOK*, PUBLISHED BY CHRONICLE BOOKS.

Heceta Head Lighthouse, Central Oregon

1st class
POSTAGE

COPYRIGHT © 1999 THEA SCHRACK/FROM *PACIFIC COAST: A PANORAMIC POSTCARD BOOK*, PUBLISHED BY CHRONICLE BOOKS.

Ruby Beach, Washington

1st class
POSTAGE

COPYRIGHT © 1999 THEA SCHRACK/FROM *PACIFIC COAST: A PANORAMIC POSTCARD BOOK*, PUBLISHED BY CHRONICLE BOOKS.

Waddell Beach, near Santa Cruz, California

1st class
POSTAGE

COPYRIGHT © 1999 THEA SCHRACK/FROM *PACIFIC COAST: A PANORAMIC POSTCARD BOOK*, PUBLISHED BY CHRONICLE BOOKS.

Haystack Rock, Cannon Beach, Oregon

1st class
POSTAGE

COPYRIGHT © 1999 THEA SCHRACK/FROM *PACIFIC COAST: A PANORAMIC POSTCARD BOOK,* PUBLISHED BY CHRONICLE BOOKS.

Guadalupe Sand Dunes, California

1st class
POSTAGE

COPYRIGHT © 1999 THEA SCHRACK/FROM *PACIFIC COAST: A PANORAMIC POSTCARD BOOK*, PUBLISHED BY CHRONICLE BOOKS.

Refugio State Beach, Santa Barbara, California

1st class
POSTAGE

COPYRIGHT © 1999 THEA SCHRACK/FROM *PACIFIC COAST: A PANORAMIC POSTCARD BOOK*, PUBLISHED BY CHRONICLE BOOKS.

Northern California Coast

1st class
POSTAGE

COPYRIGHT © 1999 THEA SCHRACK/FROM *PACIFIC COAST: A PANORAMIC POSTCARD BOOK*, PUBLISHED BY CHRONICLE BOOKS.

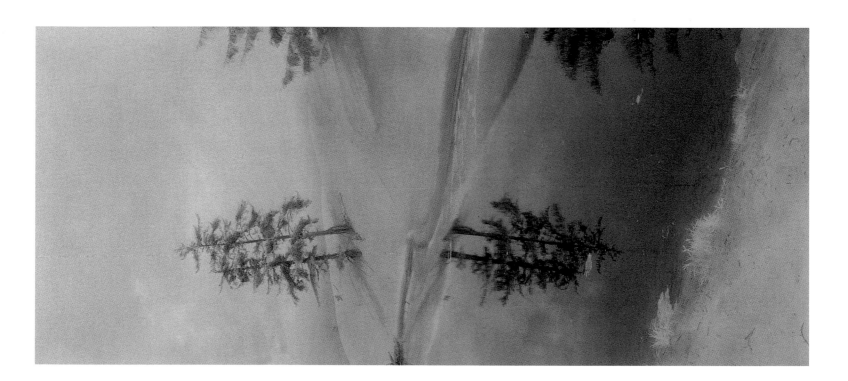

Oregon Dunes National Recreational Area

1st class
POSTAGE

COPYRIGHT © 1999 THEA SCHRACK/FROM *PACIFIC COAST: A PANORAMIC POSTCARD BOOK*, PUBLISHED BY CHRONICLE BOOKS.

Oysterville, Washington

1st class
POSTAGE

COPYRIGHT © 1999 THEA SCHRACK/FROM *PACIFIC COAST: A PANORAMIC POSTCARD BOOK*, PUBLISHED BY CHRONICLE BOOKS.

Santa Cruz, California

1st class
POSTAGE

COPYRIGHT © 1999 THEA SCHRACK/FROM *PACIFIC COAST: A PANORAMIC POSTCARD BOOK*, PUBLISHED BY CHRONICLE BOOKS.

Santa Monica, California

1st class
POSTAGE

COPYRIGHT © 1999 THEA SCHRACK/FROM *PACIFIC COAST: A PANORAMIC POSTCARD BOOK*, PUBLISHED BY CHRONICLE BOOKS.

Pigeon Point Lighthouse, California

1st class
POSTAGE

COPYRIGHT © 1999 THEA SCHRACK/FROM *PACIFIC COAST: A PANORAMIC POSTCARD BOOK*, PUBLISHED BY CHRONICLE BOOKS.

Bandon, Oregon

1st class
POSTAGE

COPYRIGHT © 1999 THEA SCHRACK/FROM *PACIFIC COAST: A PANORAMIC POSTCARD BOOK*, PUBLISHED BY CHRONICLE BOOKS.

Torry Pines, San Diego, California

1st class
POSTAGE

COPYRIGHT © 1999 THEA SCHRACK/FROM *PACIFIC COAST: A PANORAMIC POSTCARD BOOK*, PUBLISHED BY CHRONICLE BOOKS.

Sail Boats, Santa Barbara, California

1st class
POSTAGE

COPYRIGHT © 1999 THEA SCHRACK/FROM *PACIFIC COAST: A PANORAMIC POSTCARD BOOK*, PUBLISHED BY CHRONICLE BOOKS.

Newport Bridge, Newport, Oregon

1st class
POSTAGE

COPYRIGHT © 1999 THEA SCHRACK/FROM *PACIFIC COAST: A PANORAMIC POSTCARD BOOK*, PUBLISHED BY CHRONICLE BOOKS.

Huntington Beach, California

1st class
POSTAGE

COPYRIGHT © 1999 THEA SCHRACK/FROM *PACIFIC COAST: A PANORAMIC POSTCARD BOOK*, PUBLISHED BY CHRONICLE BOOKS.

Seagulls, Central Coast, California

1st class
POSTAGE

COPYRIGHT © 1999 THEA SCHRACK/FROM *PACIFIC COAST: A PANORAMIC POSTCARD BOOK*, PUBLISHED BY CHRONICLE BOOKS.

Seaside, Oregon

1st class
POSTAGE

COPYRIGHT © 1999 THEA SCHRACK/FROM *PACIFIC COAST: A PANORAMIC POSTCARD BOOK*, PUBLISHED BY CHRONICLE BOOKS.

Martinis Beach, California

1st class
POSTAGE

COPYRIGHT © 1999 THEA SCHRACK/FROM *PACIFIC COAST: A PANORAMIC POSTCARD BOOK*, PUBLISHED BY CHRONICLE BOOKS.

Huntington Beach, California

1st class
POSTAGE

COPYRIGHT © 1999 THEA SCHRACK/FROM *PACIFIC COAST: A PANORAMIC POSTCARD BOOK,* PUBLISHED BY CHRONICLE BOOKS.

Seaside, Oregon

1st class
POSTAGE

COPYRIGHT © 1999 THEA SCHRACK/FROM *PACIFIC COAST: A PANORAMIC POSTCARD BOOK,* PUBLISHED BY CHRONICLE BOOKS.